Women of Color Gratitude Journal

D Creations Publications
Dallas, TX (2021)

This journal belongs to:

____

Date:_________________

Morning!!!

Quote of the Day:____
____

This morning, I am grateful for:
____
____
____

What would make my day great:____
____
____

Morning "I AM" Affirmation:
____
____

Evening!!!!

Some amazing things that happened today:
____
____
____

What could I have done to make today even greater?________________________
____
____

What I hope tomorrow holds:____
____
____

Evening "I AM" Affirmation:____
____
____

Date:________________

Morning!!!

Quote of the Day:____
____

This morning, I am grateful for:
____
____
____

What would make my day great:______________________________
____
____

Morning "I AM" Affirmation:
____
____

Evening!!!!

Some amazing things that happened today:
____
____
____

What could I have done to make today even greater?______________
____
____

What I hope tomorrow holds:
____
____
____

Evening "I AM" Affirmation:
____
____
____

Date:_______________

Morning!!!

Quote of the Day:____
____

This morning, I am grateful for:
____
____
____

What would make my day great:_____________________________________
____
____

Morning "I AM" Affirmation:
____
____

Evening!!!!

Some amazing things that happened today:
____
____
____

What could I have done to make today even greater?___________________________
____
____

What I hope tomorrow holds:_______________________________________
____
____

Evening "I AM" Affirmation:
____
____
____

Date:_________________

Morning!!!

Quote of the Day:____
____

This morning, I am grateful for:
____
____
____

What would make my day great:_______________________________________
____
____

Morning "I AM" Affirmation:
____
____

Evening!!!!

Some amazing things that happened today:
____
____
____

What could I have done to make today even greater?___________________
____
____

What I hope tomorrow holds: ____
____
____

Evening "I AM" Affirmation:
____
____
____

Date:_________________

Morning!!!

Quote of the Day:____
____

This morning, I am grateful for:
____
____
____

What would make my day great:_______________________________________
____
____

Morning "I AM" Affirmation: ____
____

Evening!!!!

Some amazing things that happened today:
____
____
____

What could I have done to make today even greater?_________________________
____
____

What I hope tomorrow holds: ____
____
____

Evening "I AM" Affirmation:
____
____
____

Date:_________________

Morning!!!

Quote of the Day:____
____

This morning, I am grateful for:
____
____
____

What would make my day great:___________________________________
____
____

Morning "I AM" Affirmation:
____
____

Evening!!!!

Some amazing things that happened today:
____
____
____

What could I have done to make today even greater?______________
____
____

What I hope tomorrow holds: _____________________________________
____
____

Evening "I AM" Affirmation:
____
____
____

Date:_______________

Morning!!!

Quote of the Day:____
____

This morning, I am grateful for:
____
____
____

What would make my day great:____________________________________
____
____

Morning "I AM" Affirmation: _____________________________________
____
____

Evening!!!!

Some amazing things that happened today: _________________________
____
____

What could I have done to make today even greater?_______________
____
____

What I hope tomorrow holds: ______________________________________
____
____

Evening "I AM" Affirmation:
____
____
____

Date:_________________

Morning!!!

Quote of the Day:____
____

This morning, I am grateful for:
____
____
____

What would make my day great:_________________________________
____
____

Morning "I AM" Affirmation: ___________________________________
____
____

Evening!!!!

Some amazing things that happened today: _______________________
____
____

What could I have done to make today even greater?_______________
____
____

What I hope tomorrow holds: ___________________________________
____
____

Evening "I AM" Affirmation:
____
____
____

Date:_______________

Morning!!!

Quote of the Day:____
____

This morning, I am grateful for:
____
____
____

What would make my day great:________________________________
____
____

Morning "I AM" Affirmation: __________________________________
____

Evening!!!!

Some amazing things that happened today: _____________________
____
____

What could I have done to make today even greater?___________
____
____

What I hope tomorrow holds: __________________________________
____
____

Evening "I AM" Affirmation:
____
____
____

Date:_________________

Morning!!!

Quote of the Day:____
____

This morning, I am grateful for:
____
____
____

What would make my day great:___________________________________
____
____

Morning "I AM" Affirmation: ____________________________________
____

Evening!!!!

Some amazing things that happened today: _______________________
____
____

What could I have done to make today even greater?_____________
____
____

What I hope tomorrow holds: ____________________________________
____
____

Evening "I AM" Affirmation:
____
____
____

Date:___________________

Morning!!!

Quote of the Day:____
____

This morning, I am grateful for:
____
____
____

What would make my day great:____________________________________
____
____

Morning "I AM" Affirmation: ______________________________________
____

Evening!!!!

Some amazing things that happened today: _________________________
____
____

What could I have done to make today even greater?_______________
____
____

What I hope tomorrow holds: ______________________________________
____
____

Evening "I AM" Affirmation:
____
____
____

Date:_________________

Morning!!!

Quote of the Day:______________________________________
____

This morning, I am grateful for:
____
____
____

What would make my day great:____________________________
____
____

Morning "I AM" Affirmation: _______________________________
____

Evening!!!!

Some amazing things that happened today: ___________________
____
____

What could I have done to make today even greater?_______________
____
____

What I hope tomorrow holds: ______________________________
____
____

Evening "I AM" Affirmation:
____
____
____

Date:_______________

Morning!!!

Quote of the Day:____
____

This morning, I am grateful for:
____
____
____

What would make my day great:_____________________________________
____
____

Morning "I AM" Affirmation: ______________________________________
____

Evening!!!!

Some amazing things that happened today: _________________________
____
____

What could I have done to make today even greater?________________
____
____

What I hope tomorrow holds: ______________________________________
____
____

Evening "I AM" Affirmation:
____
____
____

Date:______________________

Morning!!!

*Quote of the Day:*____
____

This morning, I am grateful for:
____
____
____

*What would make my day great:*___________________________
____
____

Morning "I AM" Affirmation: _____________________________
____

Evening!!!!

Some amazing things that happened today: _______________
____
____

*What could I have done to make today even greater?*_______
____
____

*What I hope tomorrow holds:*______________________________
____
____

Evening "I AM" Affirmation:
____
____
____

Date:_________________

Morning!!!

Quote of the Day:____
____

This morning, I am grateful for:
____
____
____

What would make my day great:____
____
____

Morning "I AM" Affirmation: ____
____

Evening!!!!

Some amazing things that happened today: __________________________________
____
____

What could I have done to make today even greater?_________________________
____
____

What I hope tomorrow holds: ____
____
____

Evening "I AM" Affirmation:
____
____
____

Date:_________________

Morning!!!

Quote of the Day:____
____

This morning, I am grateful for:
____
____
____

What would make my day great:____________________________________
____
____

Morning "I AM" Affirmation: ______________________________________
____

Evening!!!!

Some amazing things that happened today: _________________________
____
____

What could I have done to make today even greater?_______________
____
____

What I hope tomorrow holds: ______________________________________
____
____

Evening "I AM" Affirmation:
____
____
____

Date:_______________

Morning!!!

Quote of the Day:____
____

This morning, I am grateful for:
____
____
____

What would make my day great:_____________________________________
____
____

Morning "I AM" Affirmation: _______________________________________
____

Evening!!!!

Some amazing things that happened today: __________________________
____
____

What could I have done to make today even greater?________________
____
____

What I hope tomorrow holds: _______________________________________
____
____

Evening "I AM" Affirmation:
____
____
____

Date:_________________

Morning!!!

Quote of the Day:____
____

This morning, I am grateful for:
____
____
____

What would make my day great:____
____
____

Morning "I AM" Affirmation: ____
____

Evening!!!!

Some amazing things that happened today: _______________________________
____
____

What could I have done to make today even greater?_______________________
____
____

What I hope tomorrow holds: ____
____
____

Evening "I AM" Affirmation:
____
____
____

Date:_______________

Morning!!!

Quote of the Day:____
____

This morning, I am grateful for:
____
____
____

What would make my day great:_____________________________
____
____

Morning "I AM" Affirmation: ________________________________
____

Evening!!!!

Some amazing things that happened today: ____________________
____
____

What could I have done to make today even greater?______________
____
____

What I hope tomorrow holds: _______________________________
____
____

Evening "I AM" Affirmation:
____
____
____

Date:_________________

Morning!!!

Quote of the Day:____
____

This morning, I am grateful for:
____
____
____

What would make my day great:___________________________________
____
____

Morning "I AM" Affirmation: ____________________________________
____

Evening!!!!

Some amazing things that happened today: ________________________
____
____

What could I have done to make today even greater?______________
____
____

What I hope tomorrow holds: _____________________________________
____
____

Evening "I AM" Affirmation:
____
____
____

Date:_______________

Morning!!!

Quote of the Day:____
____

This morning, I am grateful for:
____
____
____

What would make my day great:____
____
____

Morning "I AM" Affirmation: ____
____

Evening!!!!

Some amazing things that happened today: _______________________________
____
____

What could I have done to make today even greater?_______________________
____
____

What I hope tomorrow holds: ____
____
____

Evening "I AM" Affirmation:
____
____
____

Date:_________________

Morning!!!

Quote of the Day:______________________________________
____

This morning, I am grateful for:
____
____
____

What would make my day great:___________________________
____
____

Morning "I AM" Affirmation: _____________________________
____

Evening!!!!

Some amazing things that happened today: ________________
____
____

What could I have done to make today even greater?_______
____
____

What I hope tomorrow holds: _____________________________
____
____

Evening "I AM" Affirmation:
____
____
____

Date:_ _ _ _ _ _ _ _ _ _ _ _ _

Morning!!!

Quote of the Day:_ _
_ _

This morning, I am grateful for:
_ _
_ _
_ _

What would make my day great:_ _
_ _
_ _

Morning "I AM" Affirmation: _
_ _

Evening!!!!

Some amazing things that happened today: _ _ _ _ _ _ _ _ _ _ _ _ _ _ _ _ _ _
_ _
_ _

What could I have done to make today even greater?_ _ _ _ _ _ _ _ _ _ _ _ _ _
_ _
_ _

What I hope tomorrow holds: _
_ _
_ _

Evening "I AM" Affirmation:
_ _
_ _
_ _

Date:_________________

Morning!!!

Quote of the Day:____
____

This morning, I am grateful for:
____
____
____

What would make my day great:____
____
____

Morning "I AM" Affirmation: ____
____

Evening!!!!

Some amazing things that happened today: _________________________________
____
____

What could I have done to make today even greater?_________________________
____
____

What I hope tomorrow holds: ____
____
____

Evening "I AM" Affirmation:
____
____
____

Date:_______________

Morning!!!

Quote of the Day:____
____

This morning, I am grateful for:
____
____
____

What would make my day great:_____________________________________
____
____

Morning "I AM" Affirmation: ______________________________________
____

Evening!!!!

Some amazing things that happened today: __________________________
____
____

What could I have done to make today even greater?________________
____
____

What I hope tomorrow holds: _______________________________________
____
____

Evening "I AM" Affirmation:
____
____
____

Date:_________________

Morning!!!

Quote of the Day:____
____

This morning, I am grateful for:
____
____
____

What would make my day great:___________________________________
____
____

Morning "I AM" Affirmation: _____________________________________
____

Evening!!!!

Some amazing things that happened today: _________________________
____
____

What could I have done to make today even greater?_______________
____
____

What I hope tomorrow holds: ______________________________________
____
____

Evening "I AM" Affirmation:
____
____
____

Date:_________________

Morning!!!

Quote of the Day:____
____

This morning, I am grateful for:
____
____
____

What would make my day great:____
____
____

Morning "I AM" Affirmation: ____
____

Evening!!!!

Some amazing things that happened today: ___________________________________
____
____

What could I have done to make today even greater?__________________________
____
____

What I hope tomorrow holds: ____
____
____

Evening "I AM" Affirmation:
____
____
____

Date:_________________

Morning!!!

Quote of the Day:____
____

This morning, I am grateful for:
____
____
____

What would make my day great:____________________________________
____
____

Morning "I AM" Affirmation: ______________________________________
____

Evening!!!!

Some amazing things that happened today: __________________________
____
____

What could I have done to make today even greater?_________________
____
____

What I hope tomorrow holds: ______________________________________
____
____

Evening "I AM" Affirmation:
____
____
____

Date:_______________

Morning!!!

Quote of the Day:____
____

This morning, I am grateful for:
____
____
____

What would make my day great:___________________________________
____
____

Morning "I AM" Affirmation: _____________________________________
____

Evening!!!!

Some amazing things that happened today: _______________________________
____
____

What could I have done to make today even greater?_______________________
____
____

What I hope tomorrow holds: _____________________________________
____
____

Evening "I AM" Affirmation:
____
____
____

Date:_________________

Morning!!!

Quote of the Day:____
____

This morning, I am grateful for:
____
____
____

What would make my day great:____
____
____

Morning "I AM" Affirmation: ____
____

Evening!!!!

Some amazing things that happened today: _________________________________
____
____

What could I have done to make today even greater?_______________________
____
____

What I hope tomorrow holds: ____
____
____

Evening "I AM" Affirmation:
____
____
____

Date:_________________

Morning!!!

Quote of the Day:____
____

This morning, I am grateful for:
____
____
____

What would make my day great:____
____
____

Morning "I AM" Affirmation: ____
____

Evening!!!!

Some amazing things that happened today: _______________________________________
____
____

What could I have done to make today even greater?________________________________
____
____

What I hope tomorrow holds: ____
____

Evening "I AM" Affirmation:
____
____
____

Date:_________________

Morning!!!

Quote of the Day:____
____

This morning, I am grateful for:
____
____
____

What would make my day great:____________________________________
____
____

Morning "I AM" Affirmation: ______________________________________
____

Evening!!!!

Some amazing things that happened today: _________________________
____
____

What could I have done to make today even greater?_______________
____
____

What I hope tomorrow holds: ______________________________________
____
____

Evening "I AM" Affirmation:
____
____
____

Date:_________________

Morning!!!

Quote of the Day:____
____

This morning, I am grateful for:
____
____
____

What would make my day great:___________________________________
____
____

Morning "I AM" Affirmation: _____________________________________
____

Evening!!!!

Some amazing things that happened today: ________________________
____
____

What could I have done to make today even greater?______________
____
____

What I hope tomorrow holds: _____________________________________
____
____

Evening "I AM" Affirmation:
____
____
____

Date:_________________

Morning!!!

Quote of the Day:____
____

This morning, I am grateful for:
____
____
____

What would make my day great:____
____
____

Morning "I AM" Affirmation: ____
____

Evening!!!!

Some amazing things that happened today: ____
____
____

What could I have done to make today even greater?___________________________________
____
____

What I hope tomorrow holds: ____
____
____

Evening "I AM" Affirmation:
____
____
____

Date:_________________

Morning!!!

Quote of the Day:____
____

This morning, I am grateful for:
____
____
____

What would make my day great:____
____
____

Morning "I AM" Affirmation: ____
____

Evening!!!!

Some amazing things that happened today: _______________________________
____
____

What could I have done to make today even greater?________________________
____
____

What I hope tomorrow holds: ____
____
____

Evening "I AM" Affirmation:
____
____
____

Date:_________________

Morning!!!

Quote of the Day:____
____

This morning, I am grateful for:
____
____
____

What would make my day great:____
____
____

Morning "I AM" Affirmation: ____
____

Evening!!!!

Some amazing things that happened today: ________________________________
____
____

What could I have done to make today even greater?______________________
____
____

What I hope tomorrow holds: ____
____
____

Evening "I AM" Affirmation:
____
____
____

Date:_________________

Morning!!!

Quote of the Day:____
____

This morning, I am grateful for:
____
____
____

What would make my day great:____________________________________
____
____

Morning "I AM" Affirmation: ______________________________________
____

Evening!!!!

Some amazing things that happened today: _________________________
____
____

What could I have done to make today even greater?_______________
____
____

What I hope tomorrow holds: ______________________________________
____
____

Evening "I AM" Affirmation:
____
____
____

Date:_______________

Morning!!!

Quote of the Day:____
____

This morning, I am grateful for:
____
____
____

What would make my day great:____
____
____

Morning "I AM" Affirmation: ____
____

Evening!!!!

Some amazing things that happened today: ___________________________________
____
____

What could I have done to make today even greater?_________________________
____
____

What I hope tomorrow holds: ____
____
____

Evening "I AM" Affirmation:
____
____
____

Date:_________________

Morning!!!

Quote of the Day:____
____

This morning, I am grateful for:
____
____
____

What would make my day great:____
____
____

Morning "I AM" Affirmation: ____
____

Evening!!!!

Some amazing things that happened today: ____
____
____

What could I have done to make today even greater?_________________________________
____
____

What I hope tomorrow holds: ____
____
____

Evening "I AM" Affirmation:
____
____
____

Date:_______________

Morning!!!

Quote of the Day:____
____

This morning, I am grateful for:
____
____
____

What would make my day great:____________________________
____
____

Morning "I AM" Affirmation: ______________________________
____

Evening!!!!

Some amazing things that happened today: _________________
____
____

What could I have done to make today even greater?________
____
____

What I hope tomorrow holds: ______________________________
____
____

Evening "I AM" Affirmation:
____
____
____

Date:_____________

Morning!!!

Quote of the Day:____________________________________
____

This morning, I am grateful for:
____
____
____

What would make my day great:_______________________
____
____

Morning "I AM" Affirmation: _________________________
____

Evening!!!!

Some amazing things that happened today: _______________
____
____

What could I have done to make today even greater?_________
____
____

What I hope tomorrow holds: _________________________
____
____

Evening "I AM" Affirmation:
____
____
____

Date:________________

Morning!!!

Quote of the Day:____
____

This morning, I am grateful for:
____
____
____

What would make my day great:____________________________________
____
____

Morning "I AM" Affirmation: _____________________________________
____

Evening!!!!

Some amazing things that happened today: ________________________
____
____

What could I have done to make today even greater?______________
____
____

What I hope tomorrow holds: _____________________________________
____
____

Evening "I AM" Affirmation:
____
____
____

Date:_________________

Morning!!!

Quote of the Day:____
____

This morning, I am grateful for:
____
____
____

What would make my day great:____
____
____

Morning "I AM" Affirmation: ____
____

Evening!!!!

Some amazing things that happened today: ____
____
____

What could I have done to make today even greater?_________________________________
____
____

What I hope tomorrow holds: ____
____
____

Evening "I AM" Affirmation:
____
____
____

Date:______________________

Morning!!!

Quote of the Day:____
____

This morning, I am grateful for:
____
____
____

What would make my day great:____
____
____

Morning "I AM" Affirmation: ____
____

Evening!!!!

Some amazing things that happened today: ____________________________________
____
____

What could I have done to make today even greater?_____________________________
____
____

What I hope tomorrow holds: ____
____
____

Evening "I AM" Affirmation:
____
____
____

Date:_________________

Morning!!!

Quote of the Day:____
____

This morning, I am grateful for:
____
____
____

What would make my day great:___________________________
____
____

Morning "I AM" Affirmation: _____________________________
____

Evening!!!!

Some amazing things that happened today: ___________________
____
____

What could I have done to make today even greater?____________
____
____

What I hope tomorrow holds: _____________________________
____
____

Evening "I AM" Affirmation:
____
____
____

Date:_________________

Morning!!!

Quote of the Day:____
____

This morning, I am grateful for:
____
____
____

What would make my day great:_______________________________________
____
____

Morning "I AM" Affirmation: ____
____

Evening!!!!

Some amazing things that happened today: _________________________________
____
____

What could I have done to make today even greater?___________________________
____
____

What I hope tomorrow holds: ____
____
____

Evening "I AM" Affirmation:
____
____
____

Date:_______________

Morning!!!

Quote of the Day:____
____

This morning, I am grateful for:
____
____
____

What would make my day great:_____________________________
____
____

Morning "I AM" Affirmation: ________________________________
____

Evening!!!!

Some amazing things that happened today: ______________________
____
____

What could I have done to make today even greater?_______________
____
____

What I hope tomorrow holds: _______________________________
____
____

Evening "I AM" Affirmation:
____
____
____

Date:_______________________

Morning!!!

Quote of the Day:____
____

This morning, I am grateful for:
____
____
____

What would make my day great:____________________________________
____
____

Morning "I AM" Affirmation: ______________________________________
____

Evening!!!!

Some amazing things that happened today: __________________________
____
____

What could I have done to make today even greater?________________
____
____

What I hope tomorrow holds: _______________________________________
____
____

Evening "I AM" Affirmation:
____
____
____

Date:_________________

Morning!!!

Quote of the Day:____
____

This morning, I am grateful for:
____
____
____

What would make my day great:___________________________________
____
____

Morning "I AM" Affirmation: ____________________________________
____

Evening!!!!

Some amazing things that happened today: ________________________
____
____

What could I have done to make today even greater?______________
____
____

What I hope tomorrow holds: _____________________________________
____
____

Evening "I AM" Affirmation:
____
____
____

Date:_________________

Morning!!!

Quote of the Day:____
____

This morning, I am grateful for:
____
____
____

What would make my day great:___________________________________
____

Morning "I AM" Affirmation: _____________________________________
____

Evening!!!!

Some amazing things that happened today: _______________________________
____
____

What could I have done to make today even greater?_______________________
____
____

What I hope tomorrow holds: ___________________________________
____
____

Evening "I AM" Affirmation:
____
____
____